REFLECTIONS FROM A LIFE
OF PRAYER

REFLECTIONS FROM A LIFE OF PRAYER

GEORGE APPLETON

Edited by Ian Bennett

First published in Great Britain 1995
Society for Promoting Christian Knowledge
Holy Trinity Church
Marylebone Road
London NW1 4DU

Extracts from the Authorized Version of the Bible
(the King James Bible), the rights of which are vested in
the Crown, are reproduced by permission of the Crown's
patentee, Cambridge University Press.

Quotes from *The Revised Standard Version* of the Bible,
copyright 1946, 1952, 1971 by the Division of Christian
Education of the National Council of the Churches of
Christ in the USA. Used by permission.

Extracts from The Book of Common Prayer of 1662,
the rights of which are vested in the Crown in perpetuity
within the United Kingdom, are reproduced by
permission of Cambridge University Press,
Her Majesty's Printers.

British Library Cataloguing-in-Publication Data
A catalogue record for this book is available from the
British Library

ISBN 0–281–04804–5

Typeset by Wilmaset Ltd, Birkenhead, Wirral
Printed in Great Britain by BPC Paperbacks Ltd
Member of the British Printing Company Ltd

Contents

3 The Message of Jesus: The Kingdom Is Here

4 Parables

5 Wrestling with God

6 The Way of Love

10 At the Close of the Day

The Ministry of George Appleton

Born
20 February 1902

Deacon
1925

Priest
1926

Curate of St Dunstan,
Stepney
1925–1927

SPG Missionary, Burma
1927–1946

Married
Marjorie Alice Barrett
1929

Principal of the
Divinity School, Rangoon
1933–1936

Warden of the College of
the Holy Cross, Rangoon
1936–1941

Archdeacon of Rangoon
1943–1946

Director of Public Relations,
Government of Burma
1945–1946

Priest-in-Charge of Holy
Cross, Kokine, Rangoon
1946–1947

Vicar of St George,
Headstone, Harrow,
Middlesex
1947–1950

Secretary of the Conference
of British Missionary
Societies
1950–1957

Curate-in-Charge of
St Michael, Cricklewood
1950

Vicar of St Botolph, Aldgate
1957–1962

Archdeacon of London
1962–1963

Archbishop of Perth,
Western Australia
1963–1968

Archbishop of Jerusalem
1968–1974

Marjorie Appleton died
1982

Died
28 August 1993

Publications by George Appleton

Editor's Preface and Acknowledgements

The death of my father-in-law Bishop George Appleton, in August 1993, brought to an end very nearly three score years and ten of Christian ministry. George Appleton had helped countless people through his books, his leading of retreats and his personal ministry of friendship, counselling and spiritual direction. This ministry continued almost to the end of his life. In 1985 *The Oxford Book of Prayer* was published under his editorship; in 1990 he produced his autobiography, *Unfinished*, very much a spiritual autobiography; and until 5 September 1992 he wrote weekly meditations for *The Daily Telegraph*.

The aim of this book is to make more widely and permanently available some of the *Daily Telegraph* meditations, mostly from the last ten years of his life, and the fruit of many years of spiritual exploration and prayer, which he called 'the work of a lifetime'. I have added a number of his prayers, some so far unpublished, and others which are worth preserving as additions to the rich treasury of English prayer.

When he composed his weekly meditation he used to follow a deliberate method. He would begin with an aspect of the faith; then he would think about what sort of people might be helped by it. Next he collected together suitable material, illustrations and quotations, and finally he thought through how to put it all into words. He never wrote to display his erudition, or to make a debating point; he always wrote for people striving to know God better through prayer, and seeking to follow Christ in the circumstances of their lives. Like the householder in the gospel, who brought out of his treasure things new and old, George Appleton was not afraid to use an old story, or repeat or adapt an old prayer or text if it served his purpose. I have taken an editor's licence to follow his practice, and in a few places where necessary have amended a word, phrase, or punctuation to make what was originally prepared for quick reading over the cornflakes or in a commuter train a piece suitable for slow and prayerful reflection. I also tried to follow his example and picture the readers of this book, and I thought it would be helpful to select and arrange the meditations as a sequence. They are set out in ten themes, each of which contains a prayer and six meditations. Each theme could be used over the course of a week, starting on Sunday with the prayer as an introduction, and perhaps prayed again each day when the passage is read.

I am very grateful to Marilyn Warnick of *The Daily Telegraph* who first suggested the idea of this collection (a previous collection was published by Mowbray in 1981 under the title *Glimpses of Faith*); to SPCK for the use of the prayers on page 29 from *One Man's Prayers*, and on pages 99 and 113 from *Jerusalem Prayers for the World Today*; and to the Archivist of the Parkes Library in the University of Southampton where George Appleton's papers are now stored for the prayers on pages 1, 15, 43, 71, 85, 127, and for the Postscript.

I am also grateful to Rachel, my wife, whose sharp eyes spotted mistakes in her father's grammar and punctuation; to Diana Hanmer, George Appleton's secretary during his retirement, for much kind help, for the prayer on page 57, and for the information about his method of writing; and to Audrey Truman for her word-processing.

Most Biblical texts have been taken from the Revised Standard Version, though sometimes other translations have been used, and Psalms are quoted in their familiar Book of Common Prayer wording. Occasionally the author has used his own version. There are one or two short quotations from other writers whose origins I have been unable to trace. If I have failed to acknowledge the source of a prayer or a piece of writing which has been published elsewhere I apologise. Over four decades George Appleton wrote many books, collections of prayers and short meditations; sometimes, consciously or unconsciously, he re-used the same material, but as far as I have been able to discover the meditations and prayers, apart from what is already acknowledged, have not appeared in any of his other books.

1 The Creator and His Creation

In Every Age

O God, Creator and Lord of all,
I praise you that in every age,
> *in every culture,*
> *in every nation,*
> *in every religion,*
there have been people touched by you,
> *open to your revelation,*
> *kindled by your love,*
> *recognizing your presence everywhere,*
> *guided by your wisdom,*
> *living by your law,*
> *longing for the kingdom of your will.*
Number me, O Lord of all blessing, with these your saints,
and never let me rest until I share your love,
> *holiness and eternity.*

An Extra Dimension

All down the centuries human beings have wondered about our origin, our inner life, our ultimate goal. Those of us who profess to be religious search the Bible for clues to this mystery. We recognize that we have bodies, we are thinking and feeling beings, but somehow in our quiet moments we are still unsatisfied, searching and groping for something more.

The writer of the first chapter of Genesis has a daring insight, amounting to a revelation from outside himself, that man is made in the image of God. There is something in man that makes him different from every other created being or thing; something that we speak of as 'spirit'.

Meister Eckhart, a German mystic (*c.* 1300) says: 'There is a spirit in the soul, untouched by time and flesh, flowing from the Spirit, remaining in the spirit, itself wholly spiritual. In this principle is God, ever flowing in all the joy and glory of his actual self.' Sometimes he calls this principle the tabernacle of the soul, sometimes a spiritual light, sometimes a spark. He concludes that this is a mystery, as God is a mystery, free of all names and void of all forms.

Augustine, centuries earlier, urges us to undertake a journey of discovery: 'Seek for yourself, O man; search your true self. He who seeks shall find—but, marvel and joy, he will not find himself, he will find God; or if he find himself, he will find himself in God.'

A contemporary scholar, John Macquarrie, has helped me as I grope towards meaning and definition: 'When we speak of "spirit" in man, we are pointing to that extra dimension of being that belongs to him and that makes him more than a physical organism or a highly complicated animal.'

For myself, I have come to think of the self or soul as a seed implanted by God in each human, which needs to germinate and grow and be nourished by life from its Source, as illustrated by Jesus in the parable of the sower (Mark 4.1–20).

Work of a Lifetime

We often think of God as the Creator of the universe external to ourselves, but less often as the Creator of the universe within ourselves. This second creative act is the work of a lifetime, more even, for it will need to be continued in the life beyond this.

We see it worked out in Jesus, the prototype of what God means each of us to be. Paul speaks of being conformed to the image of God's Son, the firstborn among many brothers and sisters. Jesus often spoke of himself as the Son of Man, suggesting to me representative man, man as God meant him to be.

So we need to study the Gospels, not just dutifully reading them through or listening to passages read in church, but relevantly. I have been greatly helped by one of the traditional forms of quiet meditation, which generations of Christians have found helpful. This is carried out in three phases—Jesus before the eyes, Jesus in the heart and Jesus in the hands.

In the first phase we remember the occasion, imagine the scene, listen to the words spoken, reflect on the action taken, relate the incident described or the words said, to our situation today: Jesus before the eyes. In the second phase we express our loyalty and devotion to him and our desire to imitate him, an exercise worked out at length in Thomas à Kempis's *Imitation of Christ*, and expressed in the often repeated prayer of Brother Lawrence in his *Practice of the Presence of God*: 'Lord make me according to your heart.'

The third phase is Jesus in the hands, meaning asking myself what I am going to do as a result of this meditation, what difference is it going to make in my life, in my attitudes, in my thinking and behaviour? It is amazing what relevant thoughts and desires are put into our minds when we still our own mental activity and sink into the depths of our being, in listening and expectant silence.

We close such contemplation almost reluctantly, for we have been in touch with the risen Christ, the everliving one, whose promise to his followers was that he would be accessible and present with them, not only to the end of time but beyond.

A Long Way to God

The power of human beings over the world is always growing. Our powers of invention, achievement and endurance excite both wonder and admiration. Yet the question must be asked as to whether our inner nature is growing and deepening in a way commensurate with our control of nature outside ourselves. Are we happier, more integrated, less restless? Are we adventuring into a spiritual future, exploring the frontiers of this life into the realm of eternity beyond physical death?

Paul, with his knowledge of people in the Roman Empire, tells the Christians in Rome: 'All have sinned and fall short of God's glory.' Not only do we suffer a shortfall in glory and falling short of God's will for right living, but we also fall short of God's grace, which alone can enable us to approach anywhere near God's standards of holiness in character and righteousness in living.

Buddhists and Hindus believe that each of us needs many lives to qualify for the final bliss of Nirvana.

Christians and Jews believe that we shall still need purging and sanctifying after this present life before we are ready to stand before God and be at home in his new and eternal order. Paul recognized this when he wrote to his friends at Philippi: 'Not that I have already obtained this [i.e. the risen life of Christ] or am already perfect, but I press towards the goal, straining forward to what lies ahead.'

I sometimes use a prayer that was first prayed by Abu Bekr (d. AD 643), the father-in-law of Mohammad: 'I thank thee, Lord, for knowing me better than I know myself and for letting me know myself better than others know me. Make me, I pray thee, better than they suppose and forgive me for what they do not know.'

So I am still in a process of 'becoming', not yet having reached 'being'. I am still on the way, my creation is unfinished. In Jesus I see the perfection of humanity, yet the more I study him in the gospels and in prayer, the more I realize that there is still a long way to go.

Responsible Beings?

One of the claims of our modern era is that man has come of age and has accepted responsibility for himself and his environment. He is no longer at the mercy of circumstances.

The first page of the Bible represents God as giving him this authority: 'Be fruitful and multiply, and fill the earth and subdue it; and have dominion over every living thing.' We are now responsible for the world we live in, for the kind of society we are creating, and we can only get a united, caring world by working together.

Working together men have done some wonderful things: rivers have been diverted and dammed, deserts irrigated, epidemics prevented; shuttles take us round the earth and to the moon, population can be controlled, physical organs can be transplanted; there is the possibility of intervening in genetics, expectation of life is increased, pain controlled, death postponed—some even hope to abolish it. So modern man is tempted to think that he is all-sufficient and has no need to depend on higher powers. He thinks he can do without God.

Through radio and television we gain a knowledge of

the world and other people; we begin to realize the darker side of the global picture—wars, slums, widespread hunger, poverty and disease, racial prejudice, stateless and homeless refugees, overcrowded prisons, pollution, pornography, research restricted, hospital wards closed.

None of these is God's will, they are the work of men. We may have come of age intellectually and technologically, but has our spiritual development kept pace? Paul said that all these things are the birthpangs of a new order. Let us hope he was right.

We live in a time of tremendous change, when individual neighbourliness is being challenged to grow into corporate responsibility. We are becoming more compassionate and generous in times of disaster and emergency. However, we are not so good at finding a new order in which these emergencies need not arise.

There are voices which tell us that history will judge us. For religious people there is the more solemn thought that we are answerable to God, the Creator, Rescuer, Inspirer and Judge of all.

Hope Springs Eternal

And the Lord saw that the wickedness of man was great in the earth, and that every imagination of the thoughts of his heart was only evil continually. And it repented the Lord that he had made man on the earth and it grieved him at his heart. (Genesis 6.5–6, AV)

The writer might have been living today.

He was thinking of God in human terms, projecting on to God the feeling in his own heart; the things he would do if he were in God's place. His diagnosis of humanity was right; his understanding of God was only partial. Not the grief in the divine heart, but the divine despair. Isaiah had still to put into words his deeper insight: 'For my thoughts are not your thoughts, neither are your ways my ways.'

God never gives up hope. God never stops loving. God never abandons his eternal plan to gather every generation into the divine embrace; God forgives before ever we repent. It is the divine forgiveness that melts the human heart, rather than the penitence of the sinner winning the forgiveness of the Holy One. God is always gathering up the fragments, as Jesus said to his helpers at the banquet in the desert, always picking up the pieces, the flotsam and jetsam of humanity.

His ways are not our ways. Who would have thought that the nature of God could be so basically expressed in a man hanging on a cross with never-failing love in his heart? What Christian would have inspired Gandhi's death as a continuation of that love? What white man could have invented Martin Luther King? Who would have got the idea that a baby in a manger could express God, trusting that the very powerlessness of Bethlehem would show the strength of love?

Who else would have put it into the heart of Noah that the rainbow is the perennial symbol of hope, and that he who is pure light combines in that light all the loveliest colours of nature and art? Who would have thought that the Artist who conceived the rainbow is completely colour-blind when it comes to race, and that black is as beautiful to him as white? And vice-versa!

First and Last

'All in God's good time' is a phrase often used by Christians to explain delays in the answer to what seem to be thoroughly good prayers. I have been wondering recently whether God is responsible for the delay or man. Surely God must be always intending and willing that his good, right, and wise will shall be done? May it not be that we think that God is responsible for all the evil, pain, and disaster in the world?

I cannot think that a God who has revealed himself as the source of love could possibly be responsible for cancer. Nor can I think that a God who claims to be the Father of all would want his children to kill or maim one another by violence and war. Nor can I think that he would want to delay a single day in establishing his kingdom of justice, love and blessing.

Nor can my mind, conscience or heart agree with a dualism that believes in two more or less equally balanced spirits, one good and one evil, though I can well believe that there are evil spirits as well as evil men, and I have to admit that often I find myself almost schizophrenic between what I know to be right, true, honest, and loving, and what I know to be wrong, false, selfish, and hateful.

On the other hand I know that there is much love in the world, many good, loving people, and I believe in the ultimate victory of love, because I believe that God is the original and eternal and that evil is temporary, secondary, parasitic, something that should not be here.

Jesus was once addressed as 'good master'. He replied that God alone is good, perfectly good. If we believe that God is our creator, we must live in relationship with him. If we believe that he is father of all, we must live as brothers and sisters. If we deplore that things have gone woefully wrong, we must co-operate with him to set them right as quickly as possible. God's good time is always now.

2 The Image of the Invisible God

The Guest

O Christ my Lord,
*   you were the guest of Matthew,*
*   you were the guest of Peter,*
*   you were the guest of Simon the Pharisee,*
*   you were the guest of Zaccheus the taxgatherer,*
*   you were the guest of Mary and Martha and Lazarus,*
*   And on the cross no one's 'guest'.*
Yet now you must be my guest
*   and everyone's guest.*
Welcome dear Lord. Welcome.

A Long Way Ahead

Geologists tell us that our earth has been in existence for several thousand million years. It has been estimated that thinking man appeared only three to four million years ago. Man as a religious being is thought to be very much later that than, appearing possibly only twenty to thirty thousand years ago. Such estimates make us realize something of the patience of God, in his will to build a universe and to produce a race of God-like people.

Jesus walked the earth less than two thousand years ago. In the faith of Christians he represents ideal man, man as God meant him to be, fully thinking, loving and spiritual. St Paul speaks of him as the new Adam, the first of a new race of men, leading us into a new creation and a new order.

In biblical faith man has the possibility of God-likeness, a seed, as it were, of divinity. He is not just a product of animal creation. He is that, but he is more. God has added to him a spiritual nature or dimension, which makes him akin to God, capable of communion with God and becoming like God. There is always a struggle going on within man between these two natures, a question as to whether man will live according to his animal or spiritual ancestry.

The great insight that his early followers perceived from Jesus was that God is love, and that all who love are born of God and know God. Countless individuals have accepted this insight as a principle of personal relationship. We still have to apply it to humanity as a whole. In our age the struggle is to socialize love, to permeate the collective life of humanity with love. Jesus showed us how to do this, and the Church is called to be the pattern of the life of the world. Many of its members as well as its many critics regret that it does not yet do so.

Faith further perceives that God makes available the energy to do this. The struggle is on—for a spiritualized humanity and a love-permeated society. The Leader is a long way ahead, though still within the insight of faith. And two thousand years is a very short time!

The Initiative

A consultation with God or a confrontation with the powers of evil? The Gospels make it clear that the forty days down by the Dead Sea came from the Spirit's initiative. The spirit of evil recognized that a critical stage had been reached which must be neutralized at all costs.

At his baptism Jesus had become assured of his sonship, clear that God approved his leaving Nazareth and identifying himself with men, conscious of the inflow of divine power. Now he has to work out how he will exercise his sonship and use the power of which he has become conscious.

He wants people to know of God's love, he wants to free them for God's rule to their own lasting happiness, he wants to win the world for God and to make it more what God wants it to be. How can this be done?

Shall he use his power to provide for his own needs? To convince people by some spectacular exhibition of power?

To ally himself with some worldly or political motive?

He recognizes that these plausible suggestions are really subtle temptations to deflect him from the divine will. So he rejects them. What then does he choose? We are not told specifically. We can only deduce his choice from the rest of the story.

It looks as if, right from the start, he chose the way of love, of service, if necessary of sacrifice. If he is to convince, it must be by the way of love—persistent, unfailing love even if it means death. It is as if he could already see a cross at the end of the road.

God is always ready to take the initiative for a person's purpose in life, for the happiness and usefulness of each. We need to be quiet with him, to consult him, some time each day, occasionally for longer periods. Discovering his will, listening to his voice within ourselves, being ready to follow his lead will bring confirmation of faith and direction to life—and peace of heart.

Wanted: A New Reactor

The Christian Church in its call to work for reconciliation and peace will naturally look to its Lord for example
and inspiration. My imagination constantly goes back to
Gethsemane. Jesus has just gone through an hour of
spiritual crucifixion, in which he sweated blood, and the
agony of discovering that the cross was the Father's will,
in spite of its apparent defeat and finality. His heart is
now filled with quiet peace, and he goes forward to meet
those who have come to arrest him, armed with weapons
as if to apprehend a dangerous criminal.

Peter draws a sword and attempts a one-man rescue,
only to be rebutted by Jesus: 'Put your sword back in its
sheath: am not I to drink the cup that my Father has
given me?' Then he adds some words which show his
understanding of human nature and suggest a principle
for action: 'All who take the sword, die by the sword',
meaning that violence only breeds more violence.

Peter was no coward, but now he is hurt. Once again
he has failed to understand the mind of Jesus. He is

offended, as Jesus warned him he would be. Yet he follows the crowd to the house of the High Priest, but when challenged, his wounded heart can hold back no longer, and he bursts out 'I do not know him!', meaning, I suggest, 'I am through with him!' Not quite, for Jesus is not through with Peter. As he is led across the courtyard he must have heard Peter's repudiation, for he turns to look at him with pain and love. Peter then rushes into the darkness to weep out his penitent heart.

Jesus wants no armed bodyguard, no rescue, nor will he try to escape from the situation into which he has been pushed by the equally blind Judas. Only love and powerlessness can change this situation.

The defenceless Lord, the crucified Lord, the risen Lord is with us in our desperate global situation. He may not expect the world to accept the way of the cross, but he expects his followers to do so. The Church claims to be his body, the community of love. He surely expects it to pour love into all situations where there is no love.

Finding the Key

To many readers of the Gospels the experience of the two disciples walking from Jerusalem to Emmaus on the first Sunday after the death of Jesus is the most appealing and revealing of all the resurrection memories. They were talking together sadly of the happenings of the last few days and of the hopes aroused by one whom they regarded as a prophet from God, whose preaching and life fully exemplified that title.

As they walked and talked they felt a mysterious presence with them, who was able to explain the meaning of it all. Luke says in his account of this incident 'their eyes were kept from recognizing him', though in some strange way he seemed familiar, and spoke with a note of quiet authority.

When they arrived at their destination, the mystical stranger stayed with them and sat down with them to share the evening meal. They wondered even more when he said over the meal the usual blessing of God. Then, says Luke, 'their eyes were opened and they recognised him; and he vanished out of their sight.' Excited by this experience, and late as it was, they hurried back the seven miles to Jerusalem, to find that the same kind of thing was happening there.

In his new dimension of living Jesus was no longer limited by space and distance, duration of time and physical presence. The Emmaus experience suggests that we humans possess two kinds of sight, physical and spiritual. I remember that both were involved in Paul's experience on the Damascus road. We speak of such experiences as 'vision', meaning a new and more perceptive and convincing way of seeing.

To be able to recognize the risen Christ I need to know something about him already; I have to study the memories of his life before Good Friday and Easter. Then my spiritual eyes may be opened and I become aware of his continuing presence, sometimes spiritually felt though sometimes unrecognized, and my heart will be warmed as the hearts of the two on the Emmaus road. The most heartening fact of all is that he himself *comes*— to us!

Easter's Cosmic Force

It is a matter of great significance to Christians that on the very first day that the earliest disciples realized that Jesus was still alive and active, in his new order of being, he sent them out on his mission to the world. John in his thinking and interpretation brings Pentecost forward to Easter.

God's love and Jesus's own have been shown to the uttermost in the cross: 'Greater love has no man than this, that a man lay down his life for his friends.' Jesus has done this not only for them but also for those who would call themselves his enemies. He practises his command 'Love your enemies'. The circle of divine love includes within its circumference every sort and condition of men, everyone living at the present time, everyone who has lived in the past, everyone to be born in the countless generations of the future.

In addition to all-inclusive love the cross of Jesus shows us God's and his own unlimited forgiveness, however cruel and tragic and however often repeated sins may be. Christ's gospel has been enacted on the cross, and it is now to be lovingly proclaimed to the world. So his mission can begin at once: 'As the Father sent me, so I send you.'

The Good Friday-Easter-Pentecost good news is not only for individuals—it is for nations and groups, however hostile and embittered. The original disciples, the women at the tomb, and all who will later experience the risen Christ, are not only to be a community of love and forgiveness, they are to undertake a ministry of reconciliation, they are to be gatherers, bridge-builders, witnesses and messengers to humanity.

In death and resurrection, Jesus is released from bodily presence, space and time, to become a personal cosmic force, the spearhead of divine evolution towards the kind of world that God originally planned and is still creating, a kingdom that will be perfected at the great consummation at the end of time.

We have a gospel, a mission of love, an embassy of reconciliation—and a cosmic leader!

Unbroken Links

Christians are joyful during Eastertide for three reasons. The first is the evidence that Christ survived physical death and is the Everliving One. Second, there is the hope that we ourselves may similarly live in the spiritual and eternal dimension. Third, there is the assurance that our loved ones who have 'died', although hidden from our physical sight, are living in that divine milieu.

Jesus promised that the time was coming when the dead would hear his voice, the expectation being that he will be living and the dead also. Death is God's plan for bringing us into a new order of being, not limited by time, space and bodily presence, free from pain and growing in maturity, holiness, love and blessing. Our loved ones are in his hands; his plan for them is far better than we can imagine and desire. The love we have for them is not broken by physical death. As we progressively live in the divine milieu we can still keep in touch with them. We can be sure that they want to keep in touch with us as much as we want to keep in touch with them. Love is the one thing that never dies; it can not be killed.

The question of premature death is a problem to many. Children die of congenital disease or weakness. Millions die from starvation before they have had a chance to live a full life. Thousands die every year in road accidents. Others die through indiscriminate terrorism. Many never hear of a loving, merciful God.

I am grateful for an assurance by Father Ladislaus Boros:

No one is damned merely by chance, because he was suddenly called to eternity by an accident, or because he was born into a family where he never knew what love is and so could never understand what God himself is . . . or because he was hated, rejected, misjudged and wounded to the heart by human beings and so rebelled against everything including God.

We can trust the God and Father of the risen Jesus, who wants us all to be saved, perfected and eternally blessed. Easter joy continues.

3 The Message of Jesus: The Kingdom Is Here

The Two Kingdoms

O Christ, in yourself you are both the gospel and the kingdom;
show us how to preach good news
    to those who fight for the kingdom of this world.
Help us to proclaim your love for them
and call them in to work for the new heaven and earth
    which comes down from heaven,
so that both they and we may rejoice in your kingdom
    of righteousness, peace, and joy, which has no end,
    and worship the God who never fails,
even our creator and saviour, blessed for evermore.

The Storyteller

It looks as if Jesus took immense trouble in preparing his early message to his own people, which right from the start he intended to go out to all people and to be valid for all time. It was simple and clear, breathtaking in its assurance and hopefulness: God's great day has come, the long hoped-for era has arrived, the kingdom of God is here, change your thinking and your ways, live in its divine milieu.

His first hearers noted that he spoke as one with authority, as one who really knew what he was talking about. It was good news instead of threatening doom, love instead of fear, hope instead of depression; in short, God is with people, a never-failing spring of truth, goodness, beauty and love. The doors of heaven are open wide, the gates of hell are stormed and its prisoners freed, God opens blind eyes to see, deaf ears to hear, and hearts are opened to his entry and enlarged to love as he loves.

Jesus was always thinking how to help people to understand what he was trying to say. The Gospel writers perceived his method: it was to tell people stories from life, vivid stories of shepherds, housewives, farmers, dinner parties and wedding festivities, stories which people would remember even if they did not immediately grasp what he was saying. One day the penny would drop and they would see his deeper meaning. So Mark, the earliest Gospel writer, who probably wrote down what he heard his uncle Peter telling about his experiences with Jesus, remarks: 'With many parables he spoke the word to them, as they were able to hear it; he did not speak to them without a parable, but privately to his own disciples he explained everything.' (Mark 4.33–34)

Jesus worked on the principle that truth embodied in a tale can enter very lowly doors. He often mused 'With what can we compare the kingdom of God, or what parable shall we use for it?' (Mark 4.30) Evidently those first disciples were as slow as the crowds of hearers who gathered round Jesus, fascinated by his story-telling, yet not spotting the deeper meaning.

Priceless!

'The kingdom of heaven is like a merchant in search of fine pearls, who, on finding one pearl of great value, went and sold all that he had and bought it.' (Matthew 13.45) Just one sentence, thirty-one words—that is all, but the story of a man's trade, a parable of human search.

The merchant was an expert, he knew all about pearls, he could recognize real pearls from synthetic ones. Whenever he came across a more beautiful pearl than the ones he already had, he was willing to sell them in order to get that loveliest of all the pearls he had ever seen or dreamt of. Often he would take it out of its safe hiding-place, admire it and enjoy it, as he thought for ever.

Then one day he came across an even more beautiful pearl, but to get it he had to sell the most precious pearl hitherto and everything else he possessed. It was worth it. Now he felt he need go no further.

But the same thing happened all over again. And each time he underwent the same experience, with now ever-increasing joy and expectation.

What does this exquisite little parable say to me? First, that there are a lot of lovely pearls about. People in other religions have them as well as people in my own. I can ask them to show me theirs, and I can show them mine.

Second, the price is the same for every seeker—just all that I have got, nothing less, not a penny more.

Third, that I shall never find in this life the pearl I hope exists, the one finally and eternally beautiful and satisfying. It will only be found in God's new order of being, where God has prepared the most perfect, beautiful, never-fading treasure, which the human eye has not yet seen, nor human imagination pictured, prepared for all who are willing to accept it, which no thief can steal from me nor human suffering crush.

Small Beginnings

The kingdom of heaven is like a grain of mustard seed which a man took and sowed in his field; it is the smallest of all seeds, but when it has grown it is the greatest of shrubs and becomes a tree, so that the birds of the air come and make nests in its branches. (Matthew 13.31b–32)

Jesus often used the symbol of a seed to bring home to his hearers the meaning of the kingdom of God. The mustard seed would have been familiar to everyone. It looked dried up, hard, lifeless, but it had within it, like all seeds, a germ of life, which buried in the warm damp earth would germinate and send up a little shoot, become a plant, then a shrub and finally so big that it would classify as a tree and be recognized by birds as a safe place for nesting, laying a clutch of eggs, hatching and rearing a family of little ones. Tiny beginnings capable of enormous growth.

Any seed, said Jesus, must get into the soil, put down deep roots, not be stifled by surrounding weeds. It needs room to grow. Then in the case of a grain of corn it will produce thirty, sixty, a hundred-fold, and in the case of the mustard seed a tree, producing seeds year after year.

On another occasion he told his rural hearers: 'If you have faith as small as a mustard seed, you will say to a mountain "move to yonder place" and it will move, and nothing will be impossible to you.' Humorous hyperbole, to drive home his message.

The mountains are mountains of difficulty in the human mind—fear, anxiety, criticism from others, inertia, laziness. Given even a grain of faith they will disappear. Even to that tiny seed from the divine Sower, whose field is the heart of man, assured of its power of growth, what seemed at first sight an immovable mountain is now seen to be a molehill.

Given that faith, not only in the seed but in the Sower, the mountain of difficulty will be removed, something will turn up that was not there before, I shall be shown a way to go round it or given the strength to climb over it or the perseverance to tunnel through it. Nothing now seems impossible.

Intriguing but Elusive

There is a saying of Jesus which awakens the imagination yet somehow eludes definition: 'Except you turn and become as little children, you will never enter the kingdom of heaven'; never find the unfailing happiness which we long for, which the eternal Father-and-Mother God longs to give us.

Among those who crowded to listen to Jesus were mothers with a child in their arms, straddled on the hip or held by the hand. Such was the impression that he made upon them that they would often bring their children to him so that he might touch and bless them. His disciples, thinking that he would not want to be bothered, shushed them away only to be reproved: 'Let the little ones come to me, for of such is the kingdom of heaven.'

On one occasion Jesus took a small child standing by and looking up to him, and set him on his knee with his arm around him. One of the hymns I learnt as a child ran:

I wish that his hands had been placed on my head,
That his arm had been thrown around me,

And that I might have seen his kind look when he said,
'Let the little ones come unto me'.

The qualities of unspoiled childhood are trust, innocence, spontaneity, frankness, wonder. We think too of how children love to make a Christmas card or birthday present for their mother or father, or bring a bunch of flowers to a loved teacher. Yet we cannot remain arrested in childhood. Innocence goes, we become afraid and suspicious of others.

Wordsworth says, 'Heaven lies about us in our infancy', '. . . trailing clouds of glory do we come', but he laments the passing of this early glory, adding sadly, 'The things which I have seen I now can see no more.'

Are those vanished glories recoverable? We can 'turn', Jesus implies, not only back to lost innocence, but to receive forgiveness and grow into holiness. When love seems lost, we can discover the love and the lovableness of God. Our personal attitude to children, our social concern for their welfare, our compassion for loveless homes will keep us 'turned'.

We the Accused

Jeremiah was one of an amazing line of prophets who heard an inner voice saying: 'I appoint you a prophet to the nations, in a time of radical change, calling for new thinking and action.' Jesus heard the same divine message, and held the whole world in his heart.

In his last parable (Matthew 25.31–46) a day or two before his death he pictures all the nations being judged by God. He speaks of a 'kingdom prepared from the foundation of the world'. God's eternal plan is for the happiness of every generation, a kingdom continuing after physical death.

All in this kingdom are expected to provide food for the hungry, clothing for the naked, welcome for the homeless and the strangers, care for the sick and those imprisoned by circumstances. He says that such service will count as if it were done to himself.

Good people are surprised, for they cannot remember any time when Jesus was in need of such help, though they would eagerly have rushed to supply it. Jesus replies: 'As you did it to the least of my brethren, you did it to me.' So we are called as nations and as individuals to care for those in trouble and need, the least important, the least deserving even.

For the first time in human history we know the facts of human need, and have the resources and expertise to abolish hunger. We are told that the world can provide four times as much food as is needed to feed everyone adequately: also that if *every* nation reduced its annual expenditure on arms by 5 per cent, the war on hunger could be won in ten years. The year 2000 could be indeed a year of the Lord, if nations have the will. Welfare societies are doing magnificent work showing examples of what could be done if the nations together supply the massive resources needed.

As a father, grandfather, and prospective great-grand-father in a year or two, the figure that burns in my heart is 40,000, the number of children who die every day from hunger!

I stand in the dock, with fellow religionists, with British citizens, awaiting the Judge's verdict—and hoping for a mercifully suspended sentence.

Unfair?

I have been meditating on the parable of the workers in a vineyard. The owner had gone out in the early morning to hire men on a daily customary wage. Needing more men to do the pruning or picking the grapes, he had gone out at three-hourly intervals to take on more men. With only an hour to go he engaged a late group who were waiting on the off-chance to earn even an hour's pay (Matthew 20.1–15).

When the time came to pay the wages the owner instructed his manager to begin with the latest comers and work through to the first, and to pay the full day wage to them all. Understandably those who had worked through the whole day expected to get more, and when they received the same complained to the owner.

He pointed out that they had agreed on the wage offered, and in any case he surely had the right to use his money in whatever way he chose. Jesus did not explain his meaning, and mystified his hearers and later readers even further by adding: 'So the last shall be first, and first last.'

The message seems to me that if you will persist in thinking of God as an employer paying according to the work done, this is the kind of thing you will find him doing. In the kingdom of God you cannot earn salvation or blessing. It is all a matter of grace, his own generous giving. If you try to make rules for him, he will get round our human thinking, in some such ways as Jesus spoke of in the parable.

We may find ourselves sympathizing with those who had toiled through the hot day, but if we agree with their complaint we are placing ourselves with them outside the kingdom. I must remember the warning throughout Isaiah: 'My thoughts are not your thoughts, neither are your ways my ways.' If after a lifetime of devotion and effort I see someone converted and saved in the last days of his earthly life—the last becoming first—I must rejoice. In the kingdom, 'after you' is always the rule.

4 Parables

Blood Transfusion

Grant, O gracious Lord,
that as the bodies of sick people are saved
*   and strengthened by transfusions of blood,*
so our spirits may be renewed,
*   our courage raised,*
*   our minds enlightened*
*   by transfusions of grace and love,*
so that body, mind and spirit may enjoy the fullness of life,
and all of us take our part in creating the world of your will
*   shown to us by your perfect Son,*
*   Jesus Christ our Lord.*

The Empty Heart

Jesus was always looking for vivid human stories which would illustrate the truth he was trying to teach. One such parable was of a man with an unclean and evil spirit who by some happy experience had become healed. It seemed to him that his heart was like a room that had been swept, with all the accumulated rubbish thrown away, the floor scrubbed, the cobwebs removed and the walls dusted down, and the evil spirit that had lodged there sent packing. The room was now clean, attractive and inviting. But . . . it was empty, there was no one occupying it, he himself evidently living in some other part of the house.

The scene now changes and the banished spirit is pictured wandering restlessly to find another home. By chance he comes back to the place in which he had formerly been left free to spoil, and to his joy finds that it is empty. So he goes and finds seven other friends kindred in evil, and the whole gang become determined squatters. Jesus makes his point: 'So the last state of that man becomes worse than the first.'

The empty heart will always be at the mercy of wrong desires and evil intentions. To have seen the light, regretted the mistakes and bad habits of the past, made amendment for them, accepted God's eager forgiveness, and then fallen back into the old ways, is indeed to suffer a dangerous relapse, which unchecked can lead to the death of the spirit.

One of the poets who wrote those outpourings of the human heart which we call the Psalms, prayed: 'Make me a clean heart, O God, and renew a right spirit within me.' (BCP) Believers in God are offered a further insurance against the empty heart, namely that the Holy Spirit comes to live in the human spirit and will make his home there, if each will welcome him, be ready to be guided by him and accept his grace to live in the divine way.

Ways of Getting Lost

One of the earliest Christian writers wrote his Gospel to commend the good news to a friend or patron in the person of a Roman governor, and possibly through him to the far-flung Roman citizens. In one of its chapters Luke has put together three well-known parables—the Lost Sheep, the Lost Coin and the Lost Son.

In the first of these three parables the sheep was lost through its own foolishness. The silly sheep strayed not only from the shepherd but from the rest of the flock. The shepherd sees that the ninety-nine are safely in the fold and then goes off to search for the missing one—until he finds it. Then carrying it round his shoulders, he calls to his fellow shepherds to share his joy.

The lost coin speaks of those who are lost through accident, through no fault of their own. The housewife searches in every possible place and is overjoyed when she finds it. Lost through accident—like a child who has never known love, perhaps reluctantly cared for or neglected in the struggle to keep things going.

In the third parable the son goes away by his own choice, bored with life and perhaps seeking adventure, having persuaded his father to give him in advance the share of the family property which would be his when his father died. The father knows that he can only wait until the son comes back. Often he looks out from his farmhouse hoping against hope. Then one day he sees a tired ragged figure approaching, runs to meet him and clasps him by his arms. Not a word of reproach, nor a condition of future conduct, only an excited call to the servants to prepare a homecoming feast.

This very human story will be told as long as this world lasts, and I hope even then that it will be enacted innumerable times in the life beyond. God is like that, he has always been like that, his loving forgiving nature is unchanged.

Perhaps I would have done better to entitle my meditation 'Ways of Being Found'.

Pressing Invitation

He was often invited to parties, sometimes in the homes of respectable, religious people, occasionally in the homes of non-churchgoers, or those who were the employees of the occupying power. I get the impression that Jesus made a practice of accepting such invitations, looking round with interest at the other guests, ready to say a few words if invited to do so. He noticed how some quickly made for the places of honour.

On several occasions Jesus spoke of the kingdom of God as a banquet, one different from the customary ones where there are seldom guests of different social standing, unable to invite their hosts back.

Where God is the host people sometimes treat his invitation casually, thinking that they will come if they have nothing better to do. Luke (14.16–24) has a parable: a generous host had invited a large number of guests from the locality around. Apparently they had not declined, but when the servant went round to say that the meal was now ready, began to make excuses. One said that he had bought a piece of land and was anxious to confirm that it was 'a good buy' (a plot for retirement), another had purchased a team of oxen and wanted to try them out (a new car), a third said that he had just got married (are not wives invited as well?)—seemingly good reasons, but patently excuses.

The good host then sent his servants out to bring in any who were in need of a meal and fellowship. Even then there was still room, so he sent his servant out on the byways and round the village to press the people he met and others resting tiredly under the hedges wondering where the next meal was to come from. What a party it was in Jesus's story, what a party it will be in the realities of the kingdom.

Am I glad to be invited, or do I think that I might look in if I have got nothing better to do? Will I make my little parties like his? Will I make specially welcome lonely people, unemployed, unemployables, unlovables, not invited out of duty or in cold charity? I must leave each reader to finish the parable.

Human Analogies

As I read the Gospels I often discover sayings of Jesus which are in effect parables though not labelled as such, a whole parable contained in a sentence. One such saying is: 'If a son asks for bread will a father give him a stone, or if he asks for a fish will he give him a serpent?' (Matthew 7.9–10)

A large white pebble is like a small loaf of bread in shape and appearance, but completely different in substance. Similarly some fish are like snakes, particularly eels. The answer to Jesus's question is 'of course not'. He then makes his point: 'If you then, being evil, know how to give good gifts to your children, how much more will your heavenly Father give good things to *his* children!' He was not afraid of seeing the good things in human character and then applying them to the divine, 'only much more so'. He leads us from human parenthood to the Prototype of all parenthood.

Some 750 years before Jesus the prophet Isaiah made the same point when he heard God saying: 'Can a woman forget her sucking child, that she should have no compassion on the son of her womb? Even she may forget, yet I will not forget you.' In the teaching of Jesus the whole human race is the object of God's love, and every individual has a personal relationship with him.

Often people have come to me in sudden misfortune asking, 'What have I done that God should do this to me?' The answer of Jesus is 'nothing my dear, and in fact God has not done it', implying that God would not do a dirty trick like that. Not everything that happens is God's will. God is the author of all good things and only of good things. The writer of the first chapter of the Bible says: 'And God saw everything that he had made, and behold it was very good.' Perfectly good in fact. God is always creating good, even out of evil, bringing blessing out of misfortune.

No wonder Peter and Paul could say: 'Blessed be the God and Father of our Lord Jesus Christ!'

Spanning a Great Gulf

I have been asked to try to elucidate the spiritual meaning of the parable of the rich man and Lazarus, a far from simple task. The main point in the story seems to be that there is a real link between one's character and behaviour in this world and one's spiritual condition in the life after death.

We shall be much the same kind of people there as here unless . . . there is a drastic change within ourselves. We shall see that our life there is the consequence of our life here; what we are and do in this life determines our fate and happiness in the new order of being. So the message seems to be that as far as possible we create the future there by our actions and character here.

Dives does not seem to have a spark of regret for the heartless way in which he ignored the hunger and appalling sores of Lazarus. Even after death he thinks that he can use Lazarus for his own purposes. Abraham bids him 'remember', yet he addresses him as 'son'. Had there been any conscience about the past, things would have been different. It is good to note that with all his callous selfishness he is still a son of Abraham, so with the worst of us we are still God's children.

Another little ray of hope, the rich man wants to save his five brothers from a similar fate. May we see there just a flicker of unselfish thought for others? Yet Jesus warns that even if someone went from the dead to warn the selfish family, they would take no notice. For the failure to accept Moses' teaching of God's law of righteousness which results in life, means that if people refuse to live in the truth they already have, no further truth is likely to save them.

Another thought comes to me: when Jesus told the parable, 'the great gulf fixed' had not yet been spanned. There had been no notable 'go-between' between this world and the next, between God's heaven and the hell that we create for ourselves. His death in love, his compassion for sinners, God's resurrecting power, had not yet been effected. Now it has, and everything is different, both here and there.

Wanted: New Parables

The parables of Jesus were relevant to the thinking and living conditions of his own time. He spoke of shepherds and sheep, of farmworkers and seeds, fertility and harvests, of workers in the vineyard pruning the vines and gathering the grapes, of merchants and their business, of housewives making bread and searching for a lost coin, of kings and their banquets, of tax gatherers and social outcasts, of ostentation in synagogues, of the love of parents, of children wanting to get away from home and live their own lives, yet coming back to their roots. He knew that often a human story would be remembered, and only later the penny would drop.

If he were here in the flesh today I think he would give us equally relevant and memorable stories from our life today. I imagine that he would begin his stories in much the same way: the kingdom of God is like . . . a surgeon, told that the patient on whom he is operating is losing vitality, takes a bottle of blood from the blood bank, the same type of blood as the patient's own, and transfuses it into the bloodstream. It needs a surgeon to get all the details right.

Or the contemporary risen Christ, present everywhere with God, might say, or inspire a disciple, a radio engineer, to say: the kingdom is like a radio station which sends up impulses of energy to a layer of the atmosphere, which are reflected down, long or short wave, to the area which the message of love is to reach.

God might perhaps be likened to an eternally personal microchip, who can hold in his heart all the 4,000 million people living at present, the greater number of those of past generations, and somehow, in the timeless simultaneity of eternity, all those still to be born.

As I write these words, a warning remark of St Paul comes to my mind: 'I speak as a fool', but one hoping that wiser, more gifted and inspired people will see my gropings and produce parables that will speak directly to hearts and minds today. RSVP.

5 Wrestling with God

In the Depths of My Being

Grant, O Lord,
that when I come to you in prayer,
it may be in stillness of mind,
with my attention fixed on you alone,
opening my inmost self to your incoming,
finding you in the depths of my being,
　　where symbols and images,
　　thoughts and words,
　　　are no longer needed;
in loving communion with you,
　　my creator,
　　my saviour,
　　my ever welcome Lord.

Successful Struggle

The patriarch Jacob had two very significant dreams. The first is well known, dreamt on his first night out from home, as he ran away from his brother Esau, whom he had cheated: a comforting dream of a ladder between earth and heaven, with angels descending and ascending, bringing a blessing from God.

The second, some fifteen years later as he ran away from his father-in-law, is not so well known. He realizes he is entering Esau country, sends his brother a conciliatory message and present, and is told that Esau is approaching with four hundred men. He sends his two wives and eleven children on before him in the hope of their safety. Then all alone for the night he finds himself wrestling till dawn with a mysterious antagonist, who finally asks: 'What is your name?' His reply in the dream is 'Jacob', which means 'deceiver, twister', and he is told that from that night onward he should be called 'Israel', meaning one who has struggled with God and prevailed. The dream ends with a blessing from God and the assurance that he has seen God, face to face.

I sometimes wonder if the interpretation could be something deeper, more humbling, more radical. Not Jacob struggling with God, but God struggling with Jacob. We do not have to struggle with God in the hope that we may wrest something from him which he is unwilling to give. He is struggling with us to make us become what he wants us to be, so that getting straight with the past we may be worthy of his blessing and continued presence. The night's struggle left Jacob with a physical mark, a limp which reminded him of the night when his name and character were changed.

The two brothers were reconciled. The writer of Genesis tells us that Esau also was changed: 'Esau ran to meet him, and embraced him, and fell on his neck and kissed him, and they wept.' Perhaps there is a message and a precedent here, for both Jacob's and Esau's descendants today.

A Dream Come True

One of the earliest disciples of Jesus most interesting to me is Nathanael, who was a native of Cana, a neighbouring village of Nazareth. One day, as he sat quietly meditating under the shade of a fig tree, he saw his intimate friend Philip approaching, and with him a group. Philip excitedly whispered to him that the one whom Moses and later prophets had hoped for had now at last appeared, in the person of Jesus from Nazareth. Nathanael found it difficult to believe that the Messiah could possibly come from Nazareth, but Philip whispered, 'Come and meet him.'

Jesus may have asked Nathanael Bartholomew what he was so intently meditating on under the fig tree, and been told that it was on Jacob's dream of the angels descending and ascending to God. John, also one of the party, wants his readers to know that Jesus had the gift of looking into a man and seeing what kind of a person he was. John heard his verdict: 'a true Israelite in whom there is no guile', very different from Jacob who deceived his old father and cheated his brother.

Here was a man incapable of deception, one with no ulterior motives, no pretence, not wearing a mask to hide his real character, not one who says he does the right thing but has a wrong purpose in mind; in fact not a hypocrite, a pretender, an actor playing a part, adapting himself to every circumstance, with the intention of getting something for himself.

Strangely, the word hypocrite is only used in the Gospels. Jesus opens the sermon on the mount with a list of beatitudes, qualities which bring blessing and happiness, one of which is being pure in heart, resulting in seeing God the source of holiness and blessing. He warns his disciples against ostentation in giving, in seeking just a reputation for generosity and spirituality; he points out that God sees in secret, and to him all hearts are open, all desires known, and from him no secrets are hidden.

Jesus promised Nathanael that one day Jacob's dream would become reality, with Jesus himself bringing blessings from God and conducting souls to the divine presence.

Momentous Moment

Paul was a man of many journeys, but as he looked back it was the journey from Jerusalem to Damascus that must have seemed the most momentous. When he set out it was with proud self-confidence, ready to stamp out the heresy that a man executed as a criminal could possibly be the long-awaited Messiah. When he arrived he was blind, broken and helpless, convinced by a sudden burst of enlightenment that only he experienced and a voice that he alone heard. His new conviction and his complete surrender were both expressed in words that he spoke and his companions heard: 'What shall I do, Lord?'

That was the moment of his conversion. It is so in any life, whether it comes in some shattering spiritual experience or in a gradual growth and culminating conviction. With some it comes after a period of resistance, conscious or subconscious, like an obstinate ox wanting to go its own way and kicking against the directing pricks of its owner's goad. With others it is the glad recognition that another has been quietly and persistently at work the whole time. As I read Paul's account I also became aware of a compassion in the whole narrative: 'it is hard to kick against the pricks', and later the greeting of the apprehensive Ananias, 'brother Saul', an amazingly friendly salutation to a would-be persecutor.

It is not easy to discover the will of God; it seems to me that he expects us to work out the decisions with such spiritual wisdom as we have from our experience of his activity within us. In many cases there is no question, but a clear choice between something truthful and something false, an honest or dishonest act, something loving or unloving, a selfish or unselfish plan. The right choice is clear.

In other cases, it may be a choice between two courses, both of which seem equally good, or neither of which seems wholly right when we have to choose the better. When God has my will, my power of choice and decision, my desire, these will crystallize in a feeling of 'oughtness'. Then I know where I am and what I have to do.

Streets Ahead

This title is not a traffic direction but a colloquial way of saying that someone is far ahead of one's own assessment and of generally accepted assumption. It well describes Paul's conviction of the gap in greatness, wisdom and holiness, between Jesus and himself.

After his experience in Damascus Paul goes away to Arabia, probably to the desert near Sinai, to continue the new relationship, to reconstruct his whole life and to think out his new priorities. From now on he calls himself 'a slave of Jesus Christ' and is sent by him to one place or community after another, with his authority and gospel. 'Whose I am and whom I serve' expresses his new motivation.

Here was he, a Roman citizen, from a centre of learning, a student under one of the most famous rabbis of the day, a great traveller, with a knowledge of the world, becoming a supporter of one who came from a village in Galilee, who had only moved outside his own country on brief visits to what is now Lebanon and Jordan; who had no university degree or theological diploma; who became an itinerant preacher, without home or means of support, and was finally rejected by the rulers in Jerusalem and executed by the Romans. Yet in Paul's estimation this man became the first of a new breed of people, the central figure of the human race and the leader of mankind's progress. An amazing turn-round for Paul!

In one of his letters he says: 'I count everything as loss because of the exceeding worth of knowing Christ my Lord.' Everything else he treats as garbage, in the hope that in Christ he will find victorious living both in this present life and beyond. He speaks of the surpassing worth of Christ, and the peace of God which passes all understanding. All his letters have the same superlatives.

Paul's experience and valuation can be ours, must be ours, individually and in every congregation, parochial church council, assembly or synod: local, national or ecumenical. As he says in another letter, 'God wills to become everything to everybody.'

Recognized or Incognito?

Twenty years or more ago I read a novel about a communist dissident, whose doubts were being punished by solitary confinement, physical torture and degrading indignities. At the lowest point of hopeless pain he said he felt a mysterious presence which somehow helped him to hold out. The title of the novel was *Incognito*. That story, clearly based on personal experience, set me searching the Scriptures for interpretation and confirmation.

Moses at Sinai, realizing the difficult task of fashioning the liberated Israelites into a God-ruled people, prays: 'If thy presence go not with me do not carry us up from here.' The priest and prophet Ezekiel experienced the divine presence in exile in Babylon as assuredly as he had done earlier in Jerusalem. A psalmist could write: 'Whither shall I go then from thy presence?' (BCP) St John in exile on Patmos remembered the promise of Jesus: 'I will be with you to the end of the world', to the end of time and history and beyond. To John the human life and death of Jesus was a revelation of the nature, will and love of the eternal God.

The novelist of *Incognito* was unknowingly coming near to the conviction of St Paul: 'God is faithful and he will not let you be tempted beyond your strength, but with the temptation will also provide the way of escape, that you may be able to endure it.' We can have the same experience, wherever we go; whatever happens to us we need never be lonely, but rest assured that nothing can separate us from God's loving presence. No bars or prison walls can keep him out. Another verse from the Psalms takes this further: 'When I wake up after thy likeness I shall be satisfied with it.' (BCP) This can refer to the little sleep of death, as easy as falling asleep here and waking up there. It may also mean waking up to the fact of God's unceasing presence with us and his unfailing encouragement.

We are made conscious of both these gifts by faithful practice of quiet meditation, entering into personal relationship with God who wills to make his home not only with us but in us.

Inexorable Love

A number of thoughtful readers have written to me suggesting that I have too 'soft' a conception of God. The Bible, they rightly remind me, speaks of the wrath of God which comes upon the children of disobedience. But the wrath of God is different from the violent, revengeful, punitive anger to which we humans give way. Yet it must exist in opposition to the evil that is spoiling God's children, both the sinner himself and those who suffer from his evil acts.

It has been said that God will never let us go, because he loves us so much. However selfishly and viciously we behave, he will seek out those lost by their own foolishness, and those lost by accident or the action of others, and he will joyfully receive back those lost by their own deliberate choice, like the prodigal son.

He will never let us down, but in all the misfortunes, problems, failures and emergencies of life, his grace is freely available for us, to see us through any difficulty and recover us from any fall.

He will never let us off, not in the sense that he is forever seeking to punish us for our failings to live up to his standards, but rather that he will never be content until we become that which we are capable of becoming by his help. He will never be content with even our second-best, or give up hope of rescuing us from the seemingly bottomless pit of failure and despair.

There is an inexorable aspect of God's love, simultaneous with his intention that there shall be no sin, however heinous or often repeated, for which forgiveness is not available.

I believe that the cross of Jesus shows us that there is nothing we can do to God which he will not forgive. But the need to accept that forgiveness before it can become operative, implies a change of heart about the sins we have committed. He also tells us that God makes excuses for us: 'they know not what they do'; if they realized the pain that sin causes to God, they would not commit it. And—a text that convinces me and wins my heart—'God sent not his Son into the world to condemn the world, but that the world through him might be saved.'

6 The Way of Love

Today

Grant, O Lord, that this day may not pass
until its meaning has penetrated into my mind,
*   heart and conscience,*
and worked in me the purpose
in the mind and heart of Jesus Christ,
*   who accepted the cross*
*   as the way of love and holiness of life,*
*   and was raised to the perfection of life and being,*
*   eternity and love*
*   by you, Lord, blessed for evermore.*

Love Is the Passport

A priest friend of mine who was also a friend of a very successful businessman, who had amassed a great fortune, told me that he had one day expressed his admiration for this wealthy friend, saying how satisfied with life his success must have made him. He was rather surprised at the reply: 'Yes, I have done well, but it has taken all my attention and energy, and as a result I have lost the love of my wife and family.' Love does tend to get crowded out if we are too set on worldly motives.

A text from the Song of Songs, ascribed to Solomon, comes into my mind: 'Many waters can not quench love, neither can floods drown it. If a man offered for love all the wealth of his house, it would be utterly scorned.' (8.7) In the preceding verse the singer has said: 'Love is as strong as death.' The New Testament goes further and says that love is stronger than death.

Towards the end of life one realizes the truth of this. Love then is the only thing that matters—the love of husband or wife, of parents and children and grand-children and friends. Sickness or misfortune can be borne in the support of love.

Love is the only thing that we can take with us into God's new order. If there were heavenly officers on duty at the entrance to the new life, the only valid passport would be love. We might, in God's mercy, be allowed to enter without that passport, but many of us would not feel at home there, though doubtless there would be loving souls to take us in hand. In any case there will be loved ones there, who may have an intuition of our expected time of arrival, loved ones who will have been as eager to keep in touch with us as we with them.

Above all, there will be the opportunity of getting to know the source of all love, the divine love that holds in its embrace every created soul, in the past, living now and still to be born.

Total Demand

Devout Jews attach a little metal cylinder to the doorpost of their houses, in which four texts are placed. The first is one which Jesus selected as the first and greatest commandment of God's law and will: 'You shall love the Lord your God with all your heart, and with all your soul, and with all your strength.'

This command originated with Moses in the forty days, when he wanted to find out from the mind of God how the liberated slaves should live, both as individuals and as a nation.

It demands a totality of obedience, with the emphatic repetition of the word *all*. The heart is the very core of my being, my real self, what I really am; which nobody really knows except God, and myself if I make the effort to discover it. In the Bible the word 'soul' often means 'life'. It includes my physical life, but also my inner life, so I take it to mean everything in my life and the quality of my living. To love God with all my strength means to

74

make my will his and then to put it into practice, making him the chief value in my life, more than any other person however dear, more than valued treasure, more than any other cause or loyalty.

I am not merely commanded to obey God, but to love him. To command love seems impossible. Two thoughts help me, the first that God himself is so loving and lovable. He loves me first, my love is response to his. That love was shown to perfection in the life and death of Jesus.

The second thought is that when God commands anything he supplies the grace and ability to carry it out. If I put love for him first, I shall love my loved ones all the better, for I shall love them in his way, as he loves us. And if I love him, I shall want to spend time with him, giving him my full attention, stilling my own thoughts, so that his love can be experienced, permeate my whole being, and be available for others.

Certain Cure

Most of us try to put on a brave face in the happenings, difficulties, problems and failures of life. But inwardly we may have all kinds of fear: fear of the future, ill-health, old age, losing our money, losing a loved one, fear of those who might harm us, fear of death, fear even of God. How do we deal with fears?

The disciple who had such a loving relationship with Jesus in the few years that he knew him in life, and the many more years when he knew him as a continuing spiritual companion after his physical death, tells us that the only cure for fear is love. The chief thing he learnt from Jesus was that God is eternally love, and he saw in the life of Jesus a convincing example of love in terms of human living.

'Perfect love', he said, 'casts out fear', adding that he who fears is not perfect in love. That is an amazing diagnosis: not the one who does the frightening, but the one who is afraid is the one who has not become perfect in love.

Writers in the Bible exhort us to 'fear God', and in early times people may have been afraid of God. Gradually there emerged the idea of holy fear, more like a loving reverence which is eager to avoid anything that would grieve the loving heart of God; the Church speaks of it as a gift of the Holy Spirit.

Love towards our neighbours (and the neighbourhood now has widened to the whole of humanity) will deliver us from fear, make us mindful of their needs and eager to work for the unity of mankind. In every contact my heart must go out to meet, take an interest in, express good will towards them.

So God's perfect love delivers us from wrong fear of him and the future; our growing love for others will make us unafraid of them and disarm their fear of us. In every situation of lovelessness God wills us to insert love into it.

Tender and Tough

People sometimes think that love is a weak, sentimental thing that will give in to importunity or emotional blackmail. This is certainly not true of the inventor, the originator, the infuser of love, who is so eternally and completely loving that the New Testament expert on love, St John, could say that God *is* love, and that every human who loves, even in a poor imperfect way, is born of God and knows God.

God who is perfectly loving, good and wise, will never yield to prayer which has the aim of changing his mind. There is an inexorable love in God, a toughness that will never cease to be tender, but will never acquiesce in anything that is mean, unloving, self-centred, untruthful, or third-rate. God must be opposed to us as long as we allow such unlovely impulses to dominate us and develop into characteristics.

There is a story of an American president who, on his return from Sunday morning service, was asked by his wife, somehow prevented from accompanying him, what the sermon was about. He was a man of few words, and replied 'Sin!' Questioned further about what the preacher said, he added tersely, 'He was against it!'

Speaking humanly, God must be against us as long as we continue in the wilfulness or weakness of sin, because he sees more clearly than we do the damage that sin is doing both to the sinner and to his other children. God will never let us go because he loves us. He will never let us down in our need, but he will never let us off until we become what he wills and hopes we can become by his encouragement and help.

Yet God is always hopeful, for he has implanted in us a seed of his own Spirit, which can germinate and grow and produce a harvest of love, goodness and holiness. And he is always patiently waiting to be invited into the inmost depths of our being to inspire, to guide, rule and direct, with unfailing love, so that when our individual creation is complete it may be said: 'And God saw what he had made, and behold it was very good!'

Inner Reinforcement

If we really love people, we shall want to support them in trouble, to be concerned when they are ill, to encourage them in difficulties, to be their friend whatever happens, wanting them to be made strong in their inmost being. We can do all that if we offer ourselves as a link with the source of spiritual energy and love.

There is a connection between love and prayer. When we are ill, in grief or in trouble most of us find it difficult to pray. God can use the concern and love of others as a channel of blessing and strengthening. Intercession, as Christians call this type of prayer, is no longer a duty only, it is a spiritual operation of love with exciting possibilities.

St Paul told his friends around Ephesus how he prayed for them that they might be strengthened in their inner nature, be rooted and grounded in love, understand the mystery of Christ's love, experience that love in their hearts, and be filled with all the fullness of God (Ephesians 3.14–19). Divine love, spiritual experience, human love and the power that comes through prayer, seem to be woven into his prayer.

I recently discovered a modern prayer which I find splendidly prayable as I think of the many suffering people in the world and friends in need of spiritual strengthening. Adapted slightly it prays:

O God of love, may those for whom I am praying experience you as the God of love and a sure support. May this experience be stronger than the trouble that threatens to overwhelm them. May they so experience your love as a love that will overcome any sense of loneliness and hopelessness, even failure, and enable them to go forward with quiet trust, unfailing hope and grateful love.

When I pray, love increases, and the God of love has an uncanny habit of suggesting ways in which I may help to fulfil my own prayers. And the Church, and indeed all religious bodies, are meant to be communities of love, bringing love into every situation, particularly the seemingly loveless ones.

Eternal Essential

I was once sent a somewhat reproachful letter which began: 'You do carry on about love, do you not?'

It certainly seems vital to infuse love into loveless situations, to recognize that love is the only antidote for hatred, and to long for the continuance of love when some loved one is absent or has died.

We tend to associate love with physical presence, so it is natural to visit and tend the grave of a loved one's body, to go back in sad memory to days of rapture and warm companionship, but to equate love with physical presence is to class it with mortality. It is to freeze it in the past, to put it into a mortuary of our own, to lose oneself in the encircling gloom of grief which Cardinal Newman spoke of in a well-known hymn, without his glimpses of kindly light.

An artist friend once consulted me about his desire to portray the resurrection of Jesus in a way which would satisfy his own reaching after truth, which hitherto he had been unable to express. He was trying to portray the inexpressible, a spiritual event, through tone, colour and imagery, just as I try to express the ineffable in words.

Both of us felt the first intimation of the great event was in the minds of the women in the tomb on Easter morning, almost a whispering from spiritual witnesses: 'Why do you seek the living among the dead? He is not here, he is risen', liberated from the prison of the tomb, free to go with you wherever you go, as loving and enheartening as ever.

Love cannot die; love is eternal, for it is the essence of the Eternal, ever streaming from the heart of God, into the spiritual heart of those whom he has created in his own image, incarnating something of himself in them. We live when we love, we live when we are loved; when love ceases, spiritual and eternal life will wither. Let us hope that the withering process takes place slowly, so that we can take remedial action. In the meantime I feel urged to carry on pleading the necessity and wisdom of love.

7 The Good Life

Christ in Me

O Christ from God, O God in Christ, O Christ in me,
make me know that my deep self comes from you,
> *belongs to you,*
>> *is awakened and indwelt by you.*
Set me free to live spontaneously, lovingly, joyfully,
> *guided and strengthened by you,*
>> *in the pattern of your own human and divine life;*
O true man and true God.

Enjoying God

One of the advantages of the Christian ecumenical movement, the growing together of the Churches, is the discovery of their spiritual treasures. I shall never forget the thrill of hearing for the first time the opening question and answer of the shorter catechism of the Church of Scotland: 'What is the chief end of man? The chief end of man is to glorify God and to enjoy him for ever.' The first part of the answer is readily accepted by thoughtful Christians; it is the second part that excites me.

To enjoy God: to get to know the source of love, goodness, truth, wisdom and holiness; to become intimately acquainted with the originator of creation; to stand in wonder before the miracle of winter corn, spreading a sheen of lovely green over acres of ploughed earth; to see in the development of technology the possibility of a working week of much less than thirty-five hours, leaving us ample time to enjoy the love of family; to study man's past; to learn from the experiences of life from novels, plays, films and television; to understand and enjoy music, poetry and other forms of art; to laugh with the comedians at the incongruities of life and the idiosyncrasies of people; to play games (without 'professional' fouls); to enjoy watching fine play, whether of our own favourite team or their opponents. There is much to enjoy in life in God and in people who, with a little help from God, can be God-like in character and behaviour.

There is more: to be able to consult God in perplexity or in planning; to draw courage from him in misfortune, illness or failure; to know that he forgives; to enjoy him *for ever*, knowing that death is birth into the next stage of his providing love, not only for ourselves, but our loved ones, and also for those who die prematurely through the callousness or violence of man; to be confident that he picks up the pieces and makes them whole again.

All this enjoyment follows when I put God as my chief value, my first love, trusting that his will is always loving, good and wise, as shown most convincingly in his perfect son.

Why? How? When?

I am always grateful to Nicodemus for finding it difficult to understand what Jesus meant when he talked about being born again, how it could happen and how this new birth could result in a new kind of growth. Most of the translations of the New Testament use the phrase 'born again' but the editors of the Revised Standard Version are feeling after something deeper when they add as a marginal note the alternative 'born from above', while the Jerusalem Bible uses this phrase in the main text.

Nicodemus, a member of the governing body of Judaism, came to Jesus after dark, when the cool evening breeze was blowing as they sat on the housetop. They talked about the initial message of Jesus about the kingdom of God. Possibly Nicodemus already glimpsed that the law of God and the kingdom of God were one and the same thing.

Suddenly Jesus breaks in: 'Unless one receives a birth from above, in addition to physical birth, one will not understand let alone enter the kingdom of God.' Perhaps it was on that very evening that Nicodemus's spiritual conception took place, to be followed by a period of gestation. Later he found himself demanding a just trial for Jesus. Later still he cast his vote against condemnation, and a day or two afterwards came right out into the open when he went with Joseph of Arimathea to take down the broken body from the cross and give it an honourable burial.

I often wonder if the risen Jesus appeared to Nicodemus. I think Nicodemus would have recognized him, and Jesus would have been grateful to Nicodemus.

I need this second birth from above, the spiritual birth of which our physical birth is an analogy. Jewish friends tell me that they believe each child has three parents— father, mother and God. As soon as I accept this third parent, my birth from above takes place. Then my spiritual eyes are opened, a new motivation moves me, a new set of values takes over, I change direction, I look at my past in a different way.

I am Nicodemus; what happened in him, can and must happen in me.

Personality Dis-eases

Several years ago I was interested to hear of practical experiments being undertaken by groups of doctors, psychologists and laboratory technicians in America and Japan, to examine the effects of prayerful quiet on the output of brain energy, rate of breathing, heart beat and blood pressure.

They discovered that oxygen consumption decreases by up to 20 per cent after three minutes' quiet meditation, a result that takes five hours of sleep to achieve; the rate of heart beat decreases; breathing rate slows down; with continuous discipline, blood pressure becomes lower; and the blood lactates, which is associated with anxiety decrease.

I was particularly interested in the mention of blood pressure, having noted that every time I went to the doctor with some indisposition or for a check-up he took my blood pressure; any tendency to high pressure seems to be brought about by overwork, overhaste, overweight, overworry.

It took me some time to see that any trouble brought

about by psychological or spiritual causes could only be cured by spiritual or psychological means.

I was twice examined to discover if duodenal ulcers were what were bothering me, and warned that if worry was the cause they would return, even if they were cut out by the surgeon. I learned from a psychologist friend that many people who suffer from asthma are weighed down with the burden of life which expresses itself in breathlessness. He told me further that compulsive stealing was not always caused by dishonesty, but often by a lack of adventure and challenge in life. I also learned from him that competing claims in the psyche would, unless resolved, result in breakdown.

The spiritual significance of this empirical research became clear when I read of the advice given to her nuns by Teresa of Avila, a great teacher of prayer who lived in the sixteenth century: 'Let nothing disturb thee, let nothing dismay thee, all things pass. God never changes. Patience attains all that it strives for. She who has God finds she lacks nothing.' A quiet heart is a sure preventative and cure.

In the Shop Window?

I was cheered when I discovered again a quotation that had been niggling in my memory. It was from H. G. Wells, to the effect that there is in all of us something greater than the self of the shop window which all the world can see. Wells called it 'the self behind the frontage'.

That quotation suggested to me three selves which are expressions of our personality. Our earliest one is identified with the body. Other people recognize us by our appearance, our physical characteristics, the way we walk or talk. As they get to know us better, they realize that there is something inward, which somehow expresses itself through the outward and visible, yet not so easy to define. Most of us keep that inner self secret to ourselves, hiding our delusions of grandeur or ambition, as well as the things we think or do of which we are ashamed. H. G. Wells clearly thought that there was an innate potential of something good, even noble about this inner self. We sometimes speak of it as our better self.

The deepest self of all is the one which God wants us to be and which we can become by divine help. In the most movingly human of our Lord's stories, that of the prodigal son, Jesus pictures him as having spent all his inheritance, lost all his friends, reduced to feeding pigs and even sharing their food. Jesus adds 'when he came to himself', implying that there was still something basic left.

Nowadays people speak of improving the image we present to other people. The only credible way is by improving the inmost self. Sooner or later this will shine through. A psalmist puts the hope into a daring prayer: 'Try me, O God, and seek the ground of my heart: prove me, and examine my thoughts.' (BCP)

Wrong Adjective

People often speak of having a bad conscience, when their conscience disturbs them about some action they have committed. It would surely be more correct to speak of a good conscience, for conscience would be exercising the function for which it was implanted by God and developed by its owner.

I have found in personal experience that my conscience is more active in passing judgement on an action just committed than in warning me of the wrongfulness of an action that I am about to do. I may make excuse for my action, others may pass a lighter judgement on it than I do, but the nagging feeling persists that I was wrong to do it.

Some reflection before I act might save me from doing something which I would judge to be wrong afterwards. Of course, much depends on the standard of right and wrong by which I judge myself or others. I may be tempted to think that because others do something, that is a sufficient reason for following suit. On the other hand, if I profess to be a religious person, I should judge my actions by my conception of God.

So conscience needs to be progressively educated towards the character of the God I profess to believe in, or the standards of those I most admire. This can be done by studying the lives of our ancestors in faith and by a growing personal knowledge of God through prayer.

One thing seems certain: that is the nearer I come to God the more conscious I am of the gap between his holiness, love and goodness and my own. Then I want to cry out with Peter: 'Depart from me, for I am a sinful man, O Lord', though, like Peter, I should be dismayed if the Lord took me at my word. I am reminded of an old priest who wrote: 'Sin against law is grievous; sin against light [conscience] is more grievous; sin against love is most grievous of all.' The nearer I come to God, the more feelingly and often I find myself praying 'God be merciful to me, a sinner!'

Searching Questions

Many people will remember being urged when young to ignore emotion. We were told rather to rely on reason and will. Nowadays we are realizing that if feeling is suppressed our inner life becomes deprived and unsatisfied.

Feelings indicate what is going on in the depths of a person's being. They need to be regarded as an integral part of our personality. They are a revelation of character. We can consciously control thoughts and words, aware that we may damage our relationships or our prospects by unguarded remarks and uncontrolled emotion. So feelings give us a truer self-knowledge.

Yet we must not give unbridled expression to our feelings, but from time to time examine them. One of the psalmists subject to depression asked himself a searching question: 'Why art thou so heavy, O my soul; and why art thou so disquieted within me?' (BCP) We could do well to ask ourselves similar questions: 'Why am I angry? Why afraid? What am I so worried about? Why do I dislike A or B? Why do I try to avoid someone or some difficult situation? Why do I feel hurt?'

To recognize the truth about our feelings is half-way to setting them right.

Jesus warned us that wrong actions and words come from wrong feelings in the heart, from the very core of our being: 'Out of the heart come evil thoughts— murder, adultery, fornication, theft, false witness, slander. These are what defile a man.' (Matt. 15.19–20)

Another biblical writer spoke of the inner self as alone able to recognize and judge our feelings: 'The heart knows its own bitterness, and no stranger shares its joys.' (Proverbs 14.10)

Uncontrolled emotions also affect the body: anger may lead to blood pressure, worry to headaches and ulcers, overburden may lead to asthma, hatred to injuring others.

The prophet Samuel, seeking a king to replace Saul from the sons of Jesse, is warned by an intuition: 'Man looks on the outward appearance, but the Lord looks on the heart.' Another psalmist prayed: 'Search me, O Lord and know my heart!'

8 Prayer for the World

Compassion for All

Grant us to look with your eyes of compassion, O merciful God,
at the long travail of mankind:
> *the wars, the hungry millions,*
> *the countless refugees,*
> *the natural disasters,*
> *the cruel and needless deaths,*
> *men's inhumanity to one another,*
> *the heartbreak and hopelessness of so many lives.*
Hasten the coming of the messianic age
> *when the nations shall be at peace,*
> *and men shall live free from fear and free from want,*
> *and there shall be no more pain or tears,*
in the security of your will,
> *the assurance of your love,*
> *the coming of your kingdom.*
O God of righteousness, O Lord of compassion.

What Kind of a World?

As we look at the world at the present time our hearts must often fail. I need not enlarge upon its tragedies, its violence, its crimes, its false values. Perhaps all those things tell us that we are living in a time of great change when we need to adapt ourselves to changing conditions. The eye of faith may see in them the birthpangs of a new order. As Tennyson puts into the mouth of King Arthur conscious that his own death is near: 'The old order changeth, yielding place to new, and God fulfils himself in many ways, lest one good custom should corrupt the world.'

It could be a wholesome spiritual exercise to ask ourselves what kind of a world we long for. It would be even more hopeful and inspiring to ask: 'What kind of a world does God want? What kind of human society is he creating, and inviting us to co-operate with him in his work of creation?'

The prophet Isaiah heard the divine voice saying: 'Behold, I am doing a new thing . . . do you not perceive it?' Micah, a prophet in the countryside, looked forward to a time when nations would convert their weapons into implements of agriculture to feed a hungry world.

Paul looked forward to a time when devotion to Christ would rise above all differences of race, nationality, culture, economic rivalry, educational status, making us not only the family of man, but the family of God. When loyalty to God is our priority, each becomes a new person, looking out on the world with new eyes, not only granting to all their human rights, but also in a spirit of friendliness, goodwill and caring.

John, the most spiritual interpreter of Jesus, heard the risen Christ say: 'Look, I am making all things new.' He saw that in this new order 'they shall hunger no more . . . there shall be no more pain . . . God shall wipe away every tear', and all shall enjoy the abundant life of God's will, realizing that death becomes birth into the spiritual and eternal world.

So I pray for that new order, when all needs, material and spiritual, shall be supplied and all share in the life and love of God.

What's the Use?

Life today is so highly organized, with social and international groupings so large that many people wonder about their personal value and also about the efficacy of prayer in the tragic situations and big issues facing us. We say that the world is in a mess, that things seem to have got out of hand. God's hand as well as ours. What can the prayers of one individual, one congregation or even a widespread campaign do?

The first answer is that our prayer helps to keep the situation tied to God, so that he is not pushed out or ignored. A second clue is that these seemingly tragic and hopeless situations arise from wrong attitudes within the minds and spirits of us humans. So the struggle, as Paul tells us, is basically a spiritual one, not so much against flesh and blood but against powers that are spiritual. If such powers from some headquarters of evil or from our own degenerated nature are able to influence people, surely the powers of good from the original and eternal headquarters of right and love can do the same. The vital question is whether we are on God's side or against him.

Our common humanity is a great web of relationships in which each of us is a little knot which can communicate strength, beauty and character to the other knots around us. Jesus in one of his shortest parables added another factor: the kingdom of heaven is like yeast which a housewife took and kneaded into three measures of flour, till it all was leavened. Only the baker knows the small proportion of yeast needed for the total lump. To me this is a promise of the amazing effect of prayer and spiritual effort.

So when I pray about these world issues I am spiritually taking part in the global struggle for justice and peace. I am reminded also of two lines of a poem by Alcuin whom Charlemagne called from York to be head of his palace school:

That way is closed to war
Whose gate stands open to the stars.

So let us pray.

Weapons of Peace

There are few days when we do not learn in the media of acts of violence in different parts of the world. There are more and more localities where mugging makes people afraid to go out alone after dark or to open the door to unexpected knocks. The danger of nuclear war haunts anxious minds. Public figures need watchful guards against the assassin's bullet.

Centuries ago, when war was less destructive of life and property, the doctrine of the just war was initiated: there must be a just cause; war must be the only way of bringing about a change; there must be a properly-constituted authority; there must be the possibility of bettering the situation; the means must be appropriate to the end; reconciliation must be the ultimate goal.

There are statesmen and thinkers who warn us of 'the laws of violence'. Violence, they tell us, is continuity; once you start you cannot get away from it. Violence is reciprocity; others will do what you do to them. It is impossible to say 'so far and no further'. Violence begets violence, nothing else. Evil means defeat good ends.

Those who use violence always try to justify it. Today there are oppressive governments as well as violent revolutionaries. Yet good governments have to defend their people against lawless attackers, be quick to come to their aid when in trouble overseas, whether guilty or otherwise: all awesome responsibilities.

There are many causes of violence: a sense of injustice, intolerable living conditions, frustration and despair, as well as sometimes a less lawful rebellion against any laws, authority or discipline.

Christians and people of other faith will want to protest against what they think to be unjust, but we should do so without ill-will. St Paul spoke of the armour of God, the belt of truth, the breastplate of righteousness, the helmet of assurance in God, shoes to run towards peace, the handshield against spiritual petrol bombs, and our only sword, the wisdom that comes from God. These are the true weapons of peace. And always Christians will remember that we are entrusted with the ministry of reconciliation.

Counting the Cost

Some years ago I came across facts and figures published
by the Stockholm Institute of Peace Research which
shocked me then and haunt me still. Let me try and
summarize them, in the hope that they will shock other
minds and hearts.

In our century so far, 100 million people have died
from war—and it still has some years to run. The nations
of the world between them spend £250,000 million every
year on defence and armaments, twice as much as they
spend on health and 50 per cent more than they spend on
education. I am told that £8,000 million a year could
tackle the problem of world hunger and disease, provide
pure water for the 3,000 million people who do not have
it (and that alone would save countless lives). The £8,000
million a year would provide doctors, nurses and hos-
pitals in countries where the proportion to population is
quite inadequate. It would also secure schools for all,
decent homes for people to live in instead of slums,
shanty towns, refugee camps, and homes for those who
have no homes at all and move round in desperate search
of food, relief and shelter.

The sum of £8,000 million seems tremendous, but it is only the amount spent on armaments by all the nations together in a fortnight. The United Nations has calculated that if every nation, rich and poor, gave 0.7 per cent of its annual income, we could have a world free from hunger, disease and poverty within a generation, with people living happy and fulfilled lives, and not dying before they had a chance to live.

At present we are told that the average for all the nations is 0.37 per cent. Three Scandinavian nations reach the full 0.7 per cent, the UK gives only 0.34 per cent, and the USA with all its massive generosity gives a smaller percentage than that.

I am reminded of the parting words of Moses: 'I call heaven and earth to witness against you this day, that I have set before you life and death, blessing and curse; therefore choose life!' And the words of Jesus, the great admirer of Moses: 'I am come that they may have life and have it more abundantly.' (AV) And the overarching 'God so loved the world . . .' He still does.

Many Tributaries

The Bible writer who gives us such an authentic descrip-
tion of the nature of love, divine and human, also gives us
clues as to the operation of love in wider relationships. St
John, in exile for his faith, sees a vision of a river of water
clear as crystal, unmuddied by nature and unpolluted by
man, flowing from the throne of God into the life of the
world. On its banks grow trees yielding a crop every
month: the fruit for food, 'and the leaves for the healing of
the nations'. As we look at our world today we know how
desperately international relations need to be healed.

F. D. Maurice, who had such a deep understanding of
the kingdom of God, the rule of God in the hearts and
affairs of men, said more than a century ago:

The river of life is that which quickens, invigorates,
unites a society of men, to partake of God's likeness. The
tree of life is . . . he from whom all vital power descends
upon them . . . who makes all the outward ministrations
of his gospel and Church serviceable for the cure of the
miseries which selfishness has inflicted upon the nations.

Maurice speaks of God's gospel and God's Church. Today we are beginning to see that God's Church is wider than just the Christian Church; his good news has facets, like a cut diamond, in every tradition of faith. Today I believe that the risen, ever-present Christ might tell us to think of the gospel and the kingdom as a magnificent diamond, as well as the pearl of great price which so kindles the individual imagination.

The religions of the world are meeting as never before, talking together of their experiences, their gospels, and their ideas of the kind of world that God is creating. They are now feeling an urge to work together for human welfare, social justice and world peace, convinced that the family of man is the family of God. If religions will co-operate to rid mankind of fear, suspicion, xenophobia, national selfishness, increasing armaments and destructive use of nuclear power, what a blessing it will be to humanity. God's river of life has many tributaries.

Weep over the World

I have often stood at the spot traditionally associated with the incident of Jesus weeping over Jerusalem. One gets a heart-breakingly beautiful view across the Kidron Valley of the present city with its honey-coloured walls, with the lovely mosque of Omar, built over the rock where Abraham was willing to offer Isaac and learned that God did not want human sacrifice.

One sees also the empty precinct where once the Temple stood and the people of God offered daily worship to God and penitence for human sin. And the heart of the pilgrim is moved to tears for the city with the beautiful name, that has not yet found the way to peace.

The tears of Jesus are an expression of God's grief over the world today, with our failure, even refusal, to create the kind of world which he wants. The nations live in fear of one another, divided by ideologies, exploiting religious differences, yet conscious of the destructive power in the hands of men, which can be so quickly loosed to destroy our cities and devastate our countryside, so long as we believe that our only defence is escalation of armaments rather than agreed reduction.

We find fear mounting, violence increasing, hatred and greed not only animating the individual, but infecting all classes of society, crowds and nations, with a consequent devaluation of human life. Sometimes the hatred mounts to demonic evil, sometimes it is due to frustration at the refusal of the majority of us to create the conditions in which hatred need not arise.

Hatred is double-edged; it kills the spirit of the one who hates, as well as the bodies of those who are hated. It invites retaliation, is nuclear in its action, infectious in its proliferation. The only cure for hatred, as both the Buddha and Jesus remind us, is love.

All this hatred takes place in a contemporary world which has in its hands resources which could create conditions of peace, happiness and prosperity hardly possible in previous generations.

Only as we weep with God over the world is there any hope that we will work with him, using all our powers of heart, brain and hand, to create with him the world of his love.

9 Blessings and Challenges

Not Importunate Widows

O Christ
I used to think I had
  to keep seeking,
  to keep asking,
  to keep knocking,
    until you responded.
Now I know that I have
  only to seek and I shall find,
  only to ask and you will answer,
  only to knock and your door will
    at once be opened.
You do not demand importunity but simple faith
O gracious, self-giving Lord.

Eau de Vie

Sometimes a text from the Bible is so full of promise that it seems too good to be true. One such saying is the offer that Jesus made first to a woman of Samaria from whom he had asked for a drink of water at Jacob's well, just outside Nablus: 'Whoever drinks the water that I shall give will never be thirsty again; it will become a spring inside him, welling up with divine life.'

Jacob's well, which still today supplies abundant pure water, had been there for over two thousand years when Jesus and the woman talked together. The spring that fed it had been there for countless centuries before. The meeting took place around noon on a very hot day, on his long journey to Galilee. He was hot and tired. The water was cold and refreshing, drawn from a very deep well. All symbols of how God refreshes the tired, thirsty soul.

Not only was this spiritual water able to bring immedi- ate refreshment, but it could become a spring within the spirit of man, always available for his own needs and for others as well.

There is in the incident another offer. The disciples of Jesus had gone into the neighbouring village to buy food. When they returned they urged him: 'Rabbi, do have something to eat.' His reply showed that his thoughts were still on the reality behind the symbols: 'I have food to eat that you do not know about.' (JB) In the implication behind that reply I ask myself the question: 'What is it that keeps me going, supporting me in times of pressure, tiredness and depression?' The answer of Jesus is still the same: the good, wise, loving will of God and his supporting grace in all the ups and downs, the misfortunes and adventures of life.

Jesus stayed at Nablus for two days, and when he left the people told the woman: 'Now we believe not because of what you have told us about Jesus, but from our own experience of him.' Can I say the same?

Storm and Calm

There is an incident recorded in St Mark's Gospel dealing with the title of this meditation (4.35–41). Jesus, after a day's preaching to a crowd eager to listen to what he had to say about the kingdom of God, decided to cross to the other side of the Lake of Galilee with his most intimate disciples. Other boats followed, manned by people who wanted to hear more. Jesus was tired after the day's exertion, rested in the stern with his head on a cushion and fell asleep. While he was asleep a strong wind arose, such as often happened on the lake, but he slept on. His disciples, however, became alarmed and finally woke him and said: 'Teacher, do you not care if we perish?' To this he replied: 'Why are you afraid? Have you no faith?' Then in an authoritative tone he added: 'Peace! Be still!' His companions in the boat (and many devout generations since) assumed he was speaking to the wind and waves.

Could it not have been that they were mistaken, and that he was speaking to the fearful hearts of his disciples, the result being that they rowed with new vigour, and were soon at the other side, safe and sound?

In Luke's account of Paul's voyage to Rome as a prisoner we are told of a storm and shipwreck off the coast of Malta, in a much bigger ship and with more sailing in it. That, too, was at night, so the task of rescue was much more difficult. Paul alone kept his nerve and after some nights he urged all to new courage and hope, pleading that they take some food, with the assurance that none would perish: 'And when he had said this, he took bread, and giving thanks to God in the presence of all he broke it and began to eat. Then they all were encouraged and ate some food themselves.'

For myself I recognize that various storms arise within me, storms of fear and anxiety, sometimes impatience, anger and greed. To such inner storms the risen Lord says what he said centuries earlier to the panic-stricken disciples: 'Peace! Be still!' And if our faith and link with him are strong enough they will be followed by an unshakeable calm. You may perhaps ask: 'What if we sink and are drowned?' The answer is the same: we are still in the hands of God, if only we consent to his saving love and unceasing care.

Comforting Paradox

St Paul evidently suffered from some bodily weakness which he described as a thorn in the flesh. He prayed repeatedly for its removal, but to no effect, except for an intuition which said to him 'when I am weak, then I am strong', followed by an insight which he took to be a word from God: 'My strength is made perfect in weakness.'

What Paul is really saying is that when we most feel our own weakness, when we feel at the end of our tether, that is a very happy condition to be in, for then we have to depend on God. When human wisdom and human effort seem to be of no avail, that is just the moment for God's wisdom to guide us and God's strength to come to our rescue.

Two prayers come to my mind. The first is a verse of the nineteenth-century American hymn writer Samuel Longfellow:

Discouraged in the work of life,
Disheartened by its load,

Shamed by its failures and its fears,
  I sink beside the road;
But only let me think of thee,
  And then new hope springs up in me.

The second is a prayer from a seventeenth-century Anglican rector, Thomas Fuller:

Lord, teach me the art of patience whilst I am well, and give me the use of it when I am sick. In that day either lighten my burden or strengthen my back. Make me, who so often in my health have discovered my weakness, presuming on my own strength to be strong, in my sickness to rely solely on your assistance. Through Christ my Lord.

Paul led a very adventurous life, undergoing many hardships, often in the face of opposition and persecution. In prison towards the end of that life, and uncertain of the outcome, he revealed the secret of his faithfulness and endurance: 'I can do all things in him who strengthens me.'

Judgement and Compassion

Jesus emphasized to his disciples that they must not be censorious. He told them in his charge, which we speak of as the Sermon on the Mount, that God had sent him into the world not to condemn the world, but to save it.

We need to think out what he wanted to save us from. The New Testament gives a clear and unequivocal answer —from our sins. And Jesus promises us forgiveness of the past, a clean sheet and his constant help not to sin again.

Forgiveness is the healing of the soul, the inner self, for all of us fall tragically short of the holiness which God requires and which is possible if we desire it, put ourselves in his hands and remember that he is nearby to support us.

That does not mean that we can escape from the consequence of our sins, but that he does not inflict punishment on us. It means even more: he gives us grace to accept those consequences and to believe that our guilt has been purged. It is almost as if we had died and were now beginning an entirely new life under new management.

The spiritual judgement is a recognition of the facts of the case, without any condoning, cover-up or excuse. It can mean that we judge ourselves by the love and goodness seen in the human life of Jesus who lived in the realization of the relationship with the eternal Father, who is overflowing with love and mercy. Jesus accepted the agony of the crucifixion to prove God's unfailing love and forgiveness.

That must be the background of our attitude towards the failings of other people. We must have a truthful assessment of the situation, accompanied by genuine non-censoriousness and compassion, plus the assurance that God's mercy and compassion are infinitely greater than ours. In that way we shall hold the paradox of judgement and compassion, and be moved to pray 'God be merciful to me a sinner—also!'

The poet who wrote Psalm 85 says very simply what I have tried to say: 'Mercy and truth are met together: righteousness and peace have kissed each other.' (BCP)

Where Peace Begins

The highest praise and blessing was promised to peace-makers when Jesus described the happiness of heart which followed membership of the kingdom of God: 'How blest are the peacemakers, for God shall call them his children.' (Matthew 5.9, NEB) St Paul lists the harvest which living in the spirit produces: love, joy, peace, patience, kindness, goodness, fidelity, gentleness and self-control. What a peaceful world we would have if these standards infused by God were gratefully accepted by us humans.

The would-be peacemaker must be one with a peaceful heart, free from anger, hatred, envy, jealousy, anxiety and worry.

Some years ago I got to know a famous Buddhist monk from Vietnam. In one of his poems written during the holocaust there he wrote:

Promise me, promise me this day, while the sun is at its zenith, even as they strike you down with a mountain of hate and violence, remember, brother, man is not our enemy.

Alone again, I will go on with bent head, but knowing the immortality of love.

I learnt from eastern friends a lovely devotional 'radiation exercise'—to sit quietly and send out in turn waves of compassion, serenity, love and joy, first of all to those in my own home, then neighbours, those in my town or village, people in my own country and neighbouring countries, extending to the whole world including enemy countries, and finally to all the world of spirit. I ought to engage in this lovely practice more regularly, adding my little radiation to God's infinitely great radiation.

Jesus spoke of the legacy he was leaving to his followers: 'Peace I leave with you, my peace I give unto you.' Paul takes up the words of Jesus: 'The peace of God, which passes all understanding, will keep constant guard over your hearts and minds as they rest in Christ Jesus.' Let us gratefully accept Christ's peacekeeping legacy, which he received from the universal Father, and pass it on to our troubled world.

Up to the Summit

In the Sermon on the Mount Jesus tells his disciples how he expects them to fulfil the law and will of God, how to live it perfectly. Later in the sermon he says 'you must be perfect, as your heavenly Father is perfect', implying that if we have received a spiritual birth from above and claim to be his children, we must live up to the family spirit and tradition. Nothing will test that dedication more than Christ's command: 'Love your enemies and pray for those who persecute you.'

Enemies are more our neighbour than we think, for they occupy a great deal of our attention and often stir up strong feeling. Jesus affirmed the Jewish golden rule to love our neighbour as ourselves, and he added that his followers should love others as he loved them. The legacy of love we receive from our Father must recognize no boundaries and have no exceptions.

That may not mean that in loving one I regard as an enemy I shall find him congenial or easy to get on with, my temperament and his being factors in the relationship, but that I shall wish him well, want God's will for him and be ready to do him a good turn when one is needed.

In so doing, Paul says that I shall heap coals of fire on his head. Many people like myself find this difficult to understand. Some of us even think that this is not a respectable way of getting our own back. A friend of mine who had lived in Palestine for many years suggested that it referred to a practice of poor people in freezing cold going round with a clay pot on their heads into which charitable neighbours would place a share of their glowing coals. Paul's word 'heap' suggests a generous sharing.

It might be a good thing to begin with the second part of our Lord's command and pray for those we regard as enemies. A good prayer would be one Brother Lawrence, a lay brother in a Carmelite monastery in Paris, used to pray: 'Lord, make me according to your heart.' We could then rightly add 'and him/her/them'.

10 At the Close of the Day

Let Me Not Falter

Let me not falter, dear Lord,
*   in my faith in you;*
nor fail to trust your grace
*   at work within me;*
nor take my eyes off you,
*   the goal before me*
*   and the pattern for my life,*
O Christ my Lord.

Growing Old

I often wish that Jesus had lived to old age, so that he could have given us inspiration and example on how to live. In conversation with Peter, he showed that he was a keen observer of aged people, pointing out that young people can fend for themselves and go where they will, whereas older people have to depend on others and submit to their control.

Jesus's great disciple Paul gives us a consoling insight: 'Though our outward nature is wasting away, our inner nature is being renewed daily.' Paul implies that we can become spiritualized, that the energy of life can be conserved and transformed. He also suggests that although we may become old in body we can keep young in spirit.

Both Jesus and Paul would have known the promise of Isaiah 46.3–4: 'You have been borne by me from your birth . . . even to your old age . . . and to grey hairs I will carry you . . . I have made and I will bear; I will carry and save.' God accepts the responsibility of having created us.

That saintly thinker Theilhard de Chardin was aware of the signs of old age which mark both body and mind, the 'diminishments' he called them. He prayed: 'O God, grant that I may understand that it is you who are painfully parting the fibres of my being in order to penetrate to the very marrow of my substance and bear me away within yourself.' Theilhard continues:

God must in some way or other make room for himself, if he is to penetrate into us. In order to assimilate us in him, he must break the molecules of our being so as to re-cast us. The function of death is to provide the necessary entrance into our inmost selves. It will make us undergo the required disso-ciation. It will put us into the state needed if the divine force is to descend upon us. And in that way its fatal power to decompose and dissolve will be harnessed to the most sublime operation of life.

So death is the next stage to old age on the way to divine life. We should gladly look forward to both, and when they come accept, not refuse them, not fearfully or obstinately remain earth-bound and become fossilized, but jump hopefully and trustingly into our future with God.

A Card for All Seasons

A few years ago I received a Christmas card sent to me by some friends in an Anglican convent. It was a very small one and had only five words printed on it. On its front there was a drawing of a small flowering plant growing out of a small heap of stones. One of the nun friends had coloured the plant and its one flower in appropriate green and purple. But it was the greeting on the card that went home to the heart and imagination—just the five words 'Bloom where you are planted!' I have since sent out many copies to personal friends, not only at Christmas, but at other times in the year, each one hand-coloured by my good friends.

The inside of this folded card was left blank for a personal message of affection to each friend to whom I sent it. There was not room for a long message, so each one had to be short and to a personal point.

In a long and happy life I have been transplanted many times. It has not always been from one heap of stones to another; occasionally it has been to a little heap of more

will not fail you or forsake you. So be strong and of good courage . . . careful to do all according to the law which Moses my servant commanded you.'

Solomon when he dedicated the temple prayed: 'The Lord our God be with us, as he was with our fathers; may he not leave us or forsake us; that he may incline our hearts to him to walk in all his ways.' With Solomon as with Joshua, there seems an implied condition, that those who ask God's blessing and presence must walk in God's ways.

This is the path of safety and blessing. Yet I cannot believe that God ever forsakes anyone. We forsake him, we do things contrary to his will, we no longer go to him for guidance and inspiration, we forget his presence. He waits for us, ready to forgive, encourage, guide and bless.

At last I remember the promise of Jesus: 'According to your faith be it done to you.'

Dark Valleys

If a group of people were asked to name their favourite psalm, five out of ten would choose with conviction Psalm 23, while the other five would probably say that it was the only psalm they had ever heard, and then at weddings and funerals, which they had attended out of friendship rather than religious conviction. They might add that they rather liked it.

The verse in the psalm that appeals to most is: 'Yea, though I walk through the valley of the shadow of death, I will fear no evil: for thou art with me; thy rod and staff comfort me.' (BCP)

A Jewish rabbi points out in a commentary on the psalms that in the Hebrew original of that poem, the psalmist wrote 'through valleys of deep gloom'. The commentator adds that 'the exquisite wording "through the valley of the shadow of death" has become part of religious vocabulary, and one hesitates to interfere with it.'

What are the dark valleys that we humans have to pass through from time to time? There is a valley of grief at the death of a much loved husband or wife or child, and we can be assured that the loved ones had the divine presence with them through the valley. There is the valley of despondency in which so many people find themselves today; the divine shepherd is with them, if their eyes are open to see him. There is the valley of suffering and pain, which needs outside help to enable us to bear it. There is also the valley of the shadow of death which many refuse to think or talk about, and approach with secret fear. This is the darkest valley to many.

Death need no longer be thought of as the end. It is the journey to a different kind of being, no longer dependent on time and space and bodily presence. Not a far-distant country but a spiritual condition, the ultimate home intended for every human being; it is part of life planned by God, the eternal good, the source of energy and love.

Jesus, as he faced the crowds in Galilee, hungry to hear his words from God and about God, was heard by those near him to remark: 'I have compassion on the crowd, because they are like sheep without a shepherd.' Not unlike people today!

Look Back, Within, Ahead

The poet T. S. Eliot in his *Four Quartets* tells us that old people ought to be explorers. First of all, one looks back in memory to the journey so far, the story of one's life, the kind of person one has become, remembering the companions at each stage, trying to perceive meaning and direction.

One has the leisure to explore inner space, as exciting and even more important than exploring outer space. Dag Hammarskjöld, the former United Nations Secretary-General, in his secret meditations only discovered after his death, said of this search:

The longest journey
Is the journey inwards,
Of him who has chosen his destiny,
Who has started on his quest
For the source of his being.

The look back in memory and the look inwards may at first fill us with regret and dismay. We are tempted to think our golden age was in the past when we were actively involved in some absorbing task, or happy with a family growing up around us. There may be the hurt of 'losing' a loved one or the consciousness of mistaken decisions and actions, for which we need forgiveness from ourselves, others and God.

We cannot evade thoughts about the future, the certainty of death and of our move to a new state of being. Some will have a quiet trust, living each day as it comes, taking the crossing into the new dimension in their stride. Others will want to explore the future, learning from those who left insights before they crossed, and will live now in the values of the beyond, believing that there is an inner, imperishable life which can be entered by our willed relationship with a wise, loving and merciful creator.

Best of all, as we look back from the border of this new country our hearts should be warmed to gratitude by the memory of the love we have experienced and given, of the beauty of this present world and the goodness that has far outweighed the evil and the pain, together with the hope and faith that God has prepared even lovelier things which will surpass both our understanding and our desire.

Greeting and Farewell

Eighteen years ago I was invited by the editor of *The Daily Telegraph* to succeed Dean Walter Matthews of St Paul's in providing a Saturday religious meditation. It was impressed upon me that I was not expected to write anything political, but to give the readers of the paper some insight into 'the eternal verities'. I was only too happy to try to do this.

Now that old age has struck me forcibly I feel that, in my 91st year, I am too slow in finding a relevant and inspiring message for each week of the thirteen weeks of my alternating quarter. Now I feel that I need to prepare myself for the migration to the new order of being which cannot be far ahead, I need, as medieval devotional writers often said, to 'make my own soul'. Indeed it will be a relief to do without hearing aid, periodically stronger spectacles, false teeth and unsteady walk.

Through the ages inspired seekers of God have suspected, hoped and realized that in the depths of their being they were more than just physical, more than only temporary, wonderfully created by the eternal Spirit, who wills to share with us mortals his eternity and love.

Such a final meditation as this need not be confined to old dodderers like myself, for even the youngest confident adult, or the middle-aged at the height of their powers, will one day grow old. Then memory may recall helpful ideas and even actual words, that years later suddenly become positive and relevant.

A former Dean of York, whom I grew to know well, gave me in my younger years a prayer which I have adapted:

Lord,
I offer to you what I am,
to what you are.
I stretch up to you in desire,
my attention on you alone.
I cannot grasp you,
explain you,
describe you,
only cast myself into the depths
of your mystery.
I need to let your love
pierce the cloud of my unknowing
and warm me to hope and love,
as I wait,
available for your will
and sanctification,
dear Lord.

Postscript: A Vision for Jerusalem

In his later years George Appleton agreed to be President of the Mount of Olives Foundation which Etienne Boegner set up to create a garden of prayer on the Mount of Olives. The garden was dedicated on 26 September 1990 and George Appleton's words on that occasion express his vision for the garden and for Jerusalem, and sum up his life and ministry.

From the garden, pilgrims will look across the valley of Kidron to the old city with all its memories and associations. The further views will take in the growing, thriving new city of Jewish Jerusalem and East Jerusalem, the Arab city, with their tensions and rivalries.

The viewpoint will do more than that. It will make us think of the growth and life of cities, the organization of human society, the material welfare and the materialistic values of the human city, the pressures and noise of modern life, man's need of understanding his own inner being, and his relations with fellow men, social justice, human community and world peace. It will, we believe, remind him of the spiritual dimension of life, and the horizon of eternity over which each must one day pass.

The eyes of the spirit may be open to see the heavenly Jerusalem, the mother of us all, the final home of the human spirit, whose founder and builder is God, from which all evil and selfishness, all cruelty and injustice, all indifference, all

141

pain and suffering have been removed, and in which all mankind of all generations is gathered into the embrace of the divine love.

We who have begun to see the vision of this spiritual garden, hope that it will be a gift of the Christian churches of the world, cared for by the churches of Jerusalem; to which people from all countries will come, as they came at Pentecost, to take back with them a new understanding of God's love, his unceasing will for man's development, and a promise of things which pass man's understanding, which God has prepared, and to achieve which he calls us to be co-creators and fellow workers with him.

The work of the Lord will continue to go forth from Jerusalem carried as at the first Pentecost to people of every country, in every generation.